TOUGH RIDDLES FOR SMART KIDS

500 Riddles and Brain Teasers that Will Challenge the Whole Family

JENNY MOORE

Table of Contents

Introduction

We all like having fun. Why wouldn't we? It's boring to not have fun. A life without fun would be a poor life indeed. There are so many ways we can have fun. We can play games outside, like kicking or throwing a ball, with our friends. We can play games inside on the computer, or we can watch our favorite shows on TV. We can even tell jokes or pull pranks on people. Although those knock-knock jokes and games can get a bit old, can't they? There *is* something, though, that is always fun and never gets old: riddles and brainteasers.

There's nothing more fun than being asked a ridiculous question with a silly answer and realizing you're smart enough to figure out the answer. Riddles and brainteasers can be difficult, or they can be easy. No matter what shape, length, or form they come in, they are all fun.

The thing that's so fun about them is that you can do them alone, or you can do them with your friends and family. Take it from me, they're better when you're doing them with someone else. You can challenge your family and friends to figure out an answer before you, or you can work together on a really difficult question so your odds of finding the answer are even better.

I can't find the answers to any of these questions. That's why I want to ask for your help. I'll give you the questions, and you answer them for me. It would be great if you could help me out. These riddles can be sneaky and tricky, so it's better we work on them together. Watch out for the tongue twisters. They are especially tricky.

Are you ready to take a journey with me and solve these riddles? We can travel through the world of riddles and explore all of its secrets. There are lakes filled with rhymes and mountains of brainteasers. There are a few tongue twisters hanging from the trees and some tricky questions hiding in the bushes. This is going to be a fun trip, and I'm glad you're coming with me. Let's get started!

Chapter 1

C hapter one is probably the best place for us to start, unless you're feeling brave enough to try some of the harder riddles that lie ahead. I will warn you though, by skipping this chapter, you will be skipping some very fun and tricky riddles indeed.

Riddles are great, aren't they? I know I love them, and I can never get enough of them. I bet you're ready to prove to your friends and family who the best riddler is.

Effortless Riddles:

Question 1: What object will get wetter the more it dries?

I know this one is easy, but I'm just getting you started.

Question 2: Which letter in the alphabet has the most water in it?

You have to think about this one, but I'm sure you'll get it.

Question 3: What object do you need to break before you can use it?

I know you're thinking about sneaking a peek at the answers, but this one's easy if you think about it.

Question 4: Which of the months has 28 days in it?

This is a tricky one. Remember to always think outside the box and the answer will be easy.

Question 5: What goes up but doesn't come back down?

Do you know? Because I'm not sure. I know you're smart enough to figure it out, though.

Question 6: Why do bees hum?

That's a good question!

Question 7: What has four legs but can't walk?

That's strange. What could it be?

Question 8: If you looked inside the dictionary, which one of the words would be spelled incorrectly?

Don't look in the dictionary to find the answer. You already know it.

Question 9: What are the two things you can never have for breakfast?

I know it's not eggs and toast because I have that for breakfast all the time.

Question 10: What weighs more: a pound of bricks or a pound of feathers?

Wow! That's a really tricky one right there. Not too tricky for you, I'm sure.

Those riddles were pretty fun, and I'm sure you will find some of them a bit too easy. Don't worry though because this was just a warm-up. Now we can get into the really fun and tricky riddles. Ready, set, let's solve some riddles!

What Am I?

Question 1: I get smaller every time you use me to clean yourself. What am I?

Question 2: I have a face, but it's not like yours. I have arms, but they aren't like yours. What am I?

Question 3: The more you take from me, the bigger I get. What am I?

Question 4: I am yours, but everyone else uses me more than you do. What am I?

Question 5: I am an instrument. I can play music just like any other instrument, but you can't see or touch me. What am I?

Question 6: I have no wings, but I can still fly. What am I?

Question 7: I can go up and down as much as I want, but I can't move backwards, forwards, or side to side. What am I?

Question 8: When I am young I am tall, but the older I get the shorter I get. What am I?

Question 9: I can eat everything in my path and I breathe air, but if I drink water, I will die. What am I?

Question 10: People buy me for eating, but they never eat me. What am I?

Question 11: I never ask questions, but I am always answered. What am I?

Question 12: I am always coming, but I will never arrive. What am I?

Question 13: The more of me you take, the more of me you leave behind. What am I?

Question 14: Water comes down when it rains, but I go up when it rains. What am I?

Question 15: You can't see me or touch me, but I'm so fragile that you can break me when you speak. What am I?

Question 16: You can only keep me after you've given me away to someone else. What am I?

Question 17: If you have me, you cannot share me, but if you share me with someone else, you will no longer have me. What am I?

Question 18: You can hear me, but you cannot touch or see me. What am I?

Question 19: I have a neck, but I have no head. What am I?

Question 20: I travel all around the world, but I stay in one spot and don't move. What am I?

Phew! Those were some hard questions. Thank you for helping me find out what I was. Now, are you ready for some more riddles? I know I am.

The Tricky Ones:

Question 1: What kind of fish would chase a mouse?

A hungry one, I would say, but I'm not as smart as you are.

Question 2: What kind of table can you eat that is good for you?

Better think about this one.

Question 3: Why would someone bury their flashlight?

That is a weird thing for someone to do, but I'm sure there's a reason.

Question 4: Which of the colors can you eat?

Yuck! Who would eat a color?

Question 5: What building has the most stories?

Question 6: What is orange and sounds like a parrot when you say its name?

Question 7: What can you catch but cannot throw?

This is one of the trickiest ones so far.

Question 8: What kind of corn starts with the letter A?

Question 9: What is a box that has no lid or key but has gold inside of it?

How did the gold get in the box in the first place?

Question 10: Where in the world does Christmas come before Thanksgiving?

Question 11: What is the best cure for dandruff?

Question 12: What can go through a town and over a hill but doesn't even move?

Whatever it is, it sounds lazy to me.

Question 13: What comes out at night, even though no one called them, and disappears in the day, even though no one has stolen them?

Question 14: What can you throw away that will always come back to you?

Question 15: Why is an island similar to the letter T?

Oh, that's a good one.

Question 16: Joe's father has three sons. The two eldest sons' names are Snap and Crackle, but what is the third's name?

Do you know them? Because I don't...

Question 17: If you were my brother, but I wasn't your brother, then what would I be?

Question 18: What can you fill a room with that takes up no space?

I think this one has two answers, but I could be wrong.

Question 19: What can you hold in your left hand but not in your right hand?

Question 20: What pulls you down and never lets go of you?

Question 21: How many people are dead in a graveyard?

Question 22: How does an ocean say hello?

It must be a very friendly ocean.

Question 23: Why are teddy bears never hungry?

Question 24: What do you call someone who doesn't have all of their fingers on one hand?

Question 25: Why couldn't the sailors play a game of cards?

Question 26: Which football player would wear the biggest helmet?

Question 27: What is at the center of gravity?

Question 28: What kind of cup can't hold any liquid?

Certainly one with holes in it!

Question 29: What room has no doors, windows, or space in it?

Question 30: What do you call a fairy that hasn't taken a bath in a long time?

I told you these ones were going to be tricky, but I knew you were smart enough to figure them out! These next ones are going to need some creative thinking. Remember to always think outside the box. It's where you'll find all of the best answers!

Think Outside the Box:

Question 1: A monkey, a bird, and a squirrel are racing to get to the top of a coconut tree. Which one of them will get to the banana first?

This is a hard one!

Question 2: How can a pocket be empty but still have something in it?

Question 3: What has a foot but no legs?

What? I hope you can figure this one out because I'm lost.

Question 4: A poor person has it, a rich person needs it, and if you eat it, it will kill you. What is it?

Question 5: Can you name three days that aren't in the week?

This one makes me scratch my head.

Question 6: What falls down sometimes but never goes up?

Question 7: Mary's father has 5 daughters; Nana, Nene, Nini, Nono, and...?

Question 8: A cowboy rode into town on Friday. He stayed there for two days and two nights and left again on Friday. How did he do this?

Question 9: What do you call a joke book about eggs?

I would like to read a funny book about eggs.

Question 10: What can you find at the end of a rainbow?

It's not a pot of gold or a Leprechaun.

Question 11: What is the longest word in the dictionary?

Don't go looking at the dictionary again. Just think outside the box and you'll get it.

Question 12: What is lighter than a bird's feather, but even the world's strongest man wouldn't be able to hold it for more than a minute?

Question 13: I have wings and I have a tail, across the sky is where I sail. I have no eyes, mouth, or ears, and you control where I fly through the air. Do you know what I am?

Question 14: What can you serve but never eat?

What a strange question. It's making me hungry.

Question 15: Mr. Blue lives inside a blue house. Mr. Brown lives inside a brown house. Mr. Yellow lives inside a yellow house. Who lives inside the White house?

Question 16: There is a one-story pink house. Inside lives a pink person with a cat whose fur was pink, a fish whose scales were pink, a pink chair, a pink table, and a pink telephone. What color are the stairs?

How can someone love a color this much?

Question 17: There is a girl sitting all by herself in a dark room. There are no lights on, and it's too dark to see anything, yet this girl is reading a book. How?

Question 18: If you draw a line on a piece of paper, how can you make the line longer without touching it?

Question 19: What goes around the whole tree but never goes inside of it?

It's not a squirrel.

Question 20: What has a lot of keys but can't open any doors?

Question 21: What word has five letters but sounds like it only has one letter?

Question 22: What object starts with the letter T, has T inside it, and ends with the letter T?

Remember if you're creative enough, you'll find the answer.

Question 23: What allows you to see through a wall?

It's not x-ray vision.

Question 24: How do you say 'Racecar backwards'?

Question 25: How can you throw a ball as hard as possible and have it come back to you without bouncing off of anything?

Question 26: I scream, you scream, we all scream. What are we all screaming for?

Question 27: What did the elevator say to the floor?

Can elevators talk? That would be cool.

Question 28: What did one wall say to the other wall?

Question 29: I come in a lot of different colors and I grow bigger when I'm full. I'll float away if you don't hold on to me, and I make a really loud sound when I break. Do you know what I am?

Question 30: This thing goes up and it goes down, but it doesn't move at all. What is it?

I hope you thought outside the box enough to solve these riddles. Don't lose the box though, because you might need it for these next questions. These are funny and interesting. You're sure to laugh when you find the answer to each one.

A Laugh a Day Keeps the Doctor Away:

Question 1: What do you get when a vampire walks past a snowman?

Question 2: What do you call a snowman in the summer?

Why are there so many questions about snowmen?

Question 3: What did the baseball glove say to the baseball?

Question 4: A rooster laid an egg on the roof of a barn. Which way did the egg roll?

Question 5: What would give you the power to walk through a wall?

It's not a radioactive spider bite.

Question 6: In what room would you be safe from zombies?

Question 7: What does a snowman eat for breakfast?

Another snowman question, is this a fact book about snowmen?

Question 8: What does everyone have that is always overlooked?

Question 9: What do you call a camel with three humps?

I know you know this one.

Question 10: Why didn't the skeleton cross the road?

Those were some funny and super easy riddles, weren't they? They made me laugh so hard my sides hurt. I like snowmen by the way, they're pretty cool.

Answers:

Effortless Riddles Answers:

Question 1: A towel.

Question 2: The letter 'C'.

Question 3: An egg.

Question 4: All of them have 28 days, but most of them have more.

Question 5: Your age.

Question 6: Because they don't know the words to the song.

Question 7: A table.

Question 8: Incorrectly is spelled incorrectly.

Question 9: You can't have lunch or dinner for breakfast.

Question 10: Neither of them weigh more. They both weigh one pound.

What Am I?

Question 1: A bar of soap.

Question 2: A clock.

Question 3: A hole.

Question 4: Your name.

Question 5: Your voice.

Question 6: Time, because time flies when you're having fun.

Question 7: The temperature.

Question 8: A candle.

Question 9: Fire.

Question 10: A plate.

Question 11: A door.

Question 12: Tomorrow. It is never tomorrow. It is always today.

Question 13: Footsteps.

Question 14: An Umbrella.

Question 15: Silence.

Question 16: A promise.

Question 17: A secret.

Question 18: A voice.

Question 19: A bottle.

Question 20: A stamp.

The Tricky Ones:

Question 1: A catfish.

Question 2: A vegetable.

Question 3: Because the batteries are dead.

Question 4: Orange.

Question 5: The library.

Question 6: A carrot.

Question 7: A cold.

Question 8: Acorn

Question 9: An egg.

Question 10: In the dictionary because 'C' comes before 'T'.

Question 11: Baldness.

Question 12: Roads.

Question 13: The stars.

Question 14: A yo-yo.

Question 15: They're both in the middle of water.

Question 16: The third son is Joe! Weren't you listening?

Question 17: I would be your sister.

Question 18: Air! Another answer could be silence.

Question 19: Your right hand.

Question 20: Gravity.

Question 21: All of them.

Question 22: It waves.

Question 23: Because they're always stuffed.

Question 24: We call them normal because you have all of your fingers on two hands.

Question 25: Because the Captain was standing on the deck.

Question 26: The one with the biggest head.

Question 27: The letter V.

Question 28: A cupcake.

Question 29: A mushroom.

Question 30: Stinker Bell.

Think Outside the Box:

Question 1: Neither of them! You can't get a banana from a coconut tree.

Question 2: It has a hole in it.

Question 3: A snail.

Question 4: Nothing!

Question 5: Yesterday, today, and tomorrow.

Question 6: The rain.

Question 7: Nunu! Just kidding the fifth daughter is Mary, of course.

Question 8: The horse's name was Friday.

Question 9: A Yolk Book! Get it?

Question 10: The letter 'W'! I told you it wasn't gold.

Question 11: Smiles, because it has a mile in between each 'S'.

Question 12: His breath.

Question 13: A kite.

Question 14: A tennis ball.

Question 15: The President!

Question 16: There are no stairs in a one-story house.

Question 17: The girl is blind, and the book is written in braille.

Question 18: Draw a shorter line next to it.

Question 19: Its bark.

Question 20: A keyboard.

Question 21: Queue.

Question 22: A teapot.

Question 23: A window.

Question 24: Racecar backwards.

Question 25: You throw it up in the air.

Question 26: We all scream for ice-cream!

Question 27: "I'm coming down with something."

Question 28: "Meet you at the corner."

Question 29: A balloon!

Question 30: A staircase.

A Laugh a Day Keeps the Doctor Away:

Question 1: Frostbite!

Question 2: A puddle.

Question 3: "Catch you later!"

Question 4: Roosters don't lay eggs.

Question 5: A door!

Question 6: The living room. Get it? It's because they're dead.

Question 7: Snowflakes.

Question 8: A nose. You're always looking over it.

Question 9: Pregnant!

Question 10: Because he didn't have the guts.

Chapter 2

Fairish Riddles:

Fairish means medium or medium difficulty. So these riddles aren't going to be easy, but they aren't going to be hard, either. These next riddles are going to be kind of fair. I'm sure you'll have no problem solving them. You probably flew through the last riddles. These ones are going to be a piece of cake for you.

Question 1: Imagine you're in a room that is filling up with water. There are no doors or windows in this room. How do you get out?

Now that's a tricky one! I'm sure you can figure it out. Remember to always think out of the box. Sometimes your answer is in the question. Let's get to the rest of them...

Question 2: What do we see once in a minute, twice in a moment, but never in a thousand years?

Question 3: What do we get if we throw a stone of blue into the Sea of Red? What will the stone become?

Question 4: What do we know that can give us milk and has a horn, but is not a cow?

Question 5: What kind of tree can you carry in your hands?

Okay, these ones seem to be a little hard for me. Are you doing okay? Let's take a break and solve a few easier ones.

Question 6: What do you call a can opener that doesn't work?

Question 7: What runs around a house but does not move?

Question 8: When is a door not a door?

Question 9: Say the following: roast, boast, coast. What do you put in the toaster?

Question 10: Where can you find cities, towns, streets, and roads, but you can't find any people?

These are fun, but they're also kind of hard. They're making me scratch my head. I think I'm going to give you some hints for the really hard ones. If you're a really smart cookie, then you don't have to look at the hint. The hint is mostly for me anyway, because I'm getting really confused by some of these.

Take a Hint:

Question 1: What word is spelled wrong in every dictionary?

You know this one. Do you really need a hint?

Question 2: What can be as big as an elephant but not as heavy as one?

Hint: Everyone has one. It looks like you, and you can't see it in the dark.

Question 3: What do you throw away when you need it and bring back in when you don't want to use it?

Hint: You can only find it on the ocean.

Question 4: If you were in a race and passed the person in 2nd place, then what place would you be in?

Question 5: What has only one eye and cannot be seen out of?

Hint: You use it to sew.

Question 6: What has 88 keys but can't open any doors?

Hint: You can play it and it usually sounds nice.

Question 7: You walk into a room that has a candle, a fireplace, and a match. What would you light first?

Hint: You can't light the others without lighting the one first.

Question 8: A farmer has 17 sheep and all but nine die. How many sheep does he have left?

Hint: Remember the answer is usually in the question.

Question 9: Mt. Everest is the highest mountain in the world. Before it was discovered, what was the highest mountain in the world?

Question 10: What is full of holes but can still hold water?

Hint: We use it to clean.

Question 11: What is as hard as a rock but can melt if you put it in hot water?

That sounds like a funny rock. What kind of rock melts? Hint: It's a very cold rock.

Question 12: What has teeth but cannot chew or bite?

Hint: You use it on your hair.

Question 13: What has a lot of food but cannot eat any of it?

That doesn't sound nice. Hint: It usually keeps the food cold.

Question 14: What is as hard as a stone that grows on your body, and you use it every day?

Hint: Without it you would have to drink all your food.

Question 15: What is faster, hot or cold?

Hint: You can catch one, but you can't catch the other.

Question 16: What 5 letter word becomes shorter when you add two more letters to it?

The answer could be right in front of you.

Question 17: What is made of water, cries sometimes, but isn't wet?

Hint: It lives in the sky!

Question 18: How much dirt is in a 5-foot deep hole?

Question 19: How many animals did Moses take on the ark with him?

Question 20: Seven is an odd number. What can you do to make it even?

Hint: You have to take something away from it.

Question 21: What number has no value?

Question 22: Why, when you look for something, is it always in the last place you look?

Question 23: A man once went 8 days without sleeping. How did he do it?

Question 24: What kind of coat can you only put on when it is wet?

Hint: You don't put it on you.

Question 25: What has six faces and twenty-one eyes but cannot see at all?

It's not a blind monster. Hint: You use it to play games.

Question 26: Why is a ghost a bad liar?

Question 27: What runs but cannot walk, has a mouth but cannot talk, has a bed but does not go to sleep, has a bank but no money?

Hint: It's noisy and wet.

Question 28: What can go up a chimney when it's down, but cannot go down a chimney when it's up?

That does sound like a tricky one. Hint: It also goes up when it's raining.

Question 29: Tuesday, Sam, and Peter went to the restaurant to eat lunch. After they ate, they paid the bill. Sam and Peter didn't pay the bill, so who did?

The answer is in the question. Read carefully.

Question 30: A truck driver was driving down the road. His lights weren't on and the moon was not out. There was a woman up ahead, crossing the road. How did he see her?

That was pretty hard. I hope the hints helped you a little bit. If you didn't use the hints then well done for being so smart. I couldn't figure out the answers even with the hints. Let's move on to some more. I need your help figuring out what these things are.

What Is It?

Question 1: The more of it there is, the less you see. What is it?

Question 2: Everyone has one, and no one can lose it even if they try. What is it?

Question 3: Someone makes it but doesn't want it. Someone buys it but doesn't use it. The person who is using it doesn't know that they are. What is it?

Question 4: This seven letter word is spelled the same way forwards and backwards. What is it?

Question 5: It is as flat as a leaf, as round as a ring, has two eyes but can't see a thing. What is it?

Question 6: It has no body and no nose. What is it?

Question 7: It runs, but it has no legs. What is it?

Question 8: It comes in one color, but it also comes in many. Stuck at the bottom and yet easily flies. It's here in the sun but not in the rain. It does no harm and feels no pain. What is it?

Question 9: It has a long neck and shares the same name as a bird. It works all day long by the sea, but it doesn't need to eat or sleep. What is it?

Question 10: It has hands but cannot clap. What is it?

Question 11: I'll give you two clues for this one. It can be green, black, and even sweet. It sounds like one letter, but the word is spelled with three. What is it?

Question 12: You see it every day, but it is out of your reach. What is it?

Question 13: It falls but never breaks. What is it?

Question 14: It breaks but never falls. What is it?

Question 15: It floats like a log and it looks like a log, but it isn't a log. What is it?

Question 16: It's been around for millions of years, floating in the sky, but it's not even one month old. What is it?

Question 17: It doesn't bark or bite or carry a knife, but if you try to get inside, it will stop you. What is it?

Question 18: This white bird only flies when it's really cold and dies when it's hot. What is it?

Question 19: This thing is empty on the inside and as light as a feather, but ten men wouldn't be able to lift it up. What is it?

Question 20: It's all around us, but we cannot see it. We can hear it and feel it but cannot hold it. What is it?

Question 21: It doesn't get to choose whether it goes out or stays in. What is it?

Question 22: If you take off its skin, you won't hurt it, but you'll end up crying. What is it?

Question 23: It begins when things end and ends when things begin. What is it?

Question 24: As an object, it is good at measuring things. When it's a person, it is usually in charge of things. What is it?

Question 25: This is the least spoken language in the world. What is it?

Question 26: This object makes two people out of one. What is it?

Question 27: When it is black, it is clean, but when it is white, it is dirty. What is it?

Question 28: It has no wings but can fly high up into the sky. It looks like a black cloud, but rain never pours from it. What is it?

Question 29: It has four fingers and a thumb, but it has no bones, skin, or blood. What is it?

Question 30: It looks like a cat, acts like a cat, but it isn't a cat. What is it?

Those were some fun riddles. You probably worked really hard to solve them all by yourself without any hints. Let's take a break and look at some more fun riddles. These questions have some funny answers, but you still have to think out of the box to figure them out. You'll think you know the answer to these ones, but you better think again.

Think Twice Before You Answer:

Question 1: Why is Peter Pan always flying?

Question 2: What is the end of everything?

Question 3: Why did the teacher wear sunglasses to class?

Question 4: Why did the student bring a ladder to school?

Question 5: What kind of goose would fight a snake?

Question 6: Which question can never be answered with a yes?

Question 7: Why didn't the skeleton want to go to the ball?

Question 8: Why did the man throw the butter out of the window?

Question 9: How do spiders communicate?

Question 10: A boy fell off of a 100-foot ladder, but he didn't get hurt. How?

Question 11: Why did the cookie go to see a doctor?

Question 12: Why did the spider get a job in I.T.?

Question 13: What has a hundred feet in the air but has its back on the ground?

Question 14: I am a riddle, but my answer is gone. Find it for me, you have until dawn. What is it?

Question 15: Which word does not belong here: First, second, third, forth, fifth, sixth, seventh, and eighth?

Question 16: Why couldn't the little boy go and see the pirate movie?

Question 17: Why did the man hold a shoe to his ear?

Question 18: What is full during the day and empty at night?

Question 19: What do you get when you mix a duck, a beaver, and an otter together?

Question 20: What has every color in the rainbow no matter what?

Question 21: This blade is sharp, green, and slim. It can cut the wind but nothing else. What is it?

Question 22: I have a bee in my hand. What do I have in my eye?

Question 23: What is usually green, can fly, and copies others' words?

Question 24: What uses its ear to speak and its mouth to hear?

Question 25: What's a shower without water that only mommies can have?

Question 26: What grows upward and can't come back down?

Question 27: How far can a rabbit run into the woods?

Question 28: I will throw away the outside, then I can cook the inside. Once it is cooked, I can eat the outside and then I will throw away the inside. What am I eating?

Question 29: What has a bottom at the top?

Question 30: What's black and white and pink all over?

Those were some short and sweet riddles. I hope a few of them made you laugh and all of them made you think. That's the best way to think, if you ask me.

I think you're ready for some proper brain teasers. Don't worry, if they're too hard I'll give you a little hint, but I'm sure you won't need any hints.

Long Riddles:

Question 1: On a sunny day, the captain had his ship docked in the harbor. All of a sudden, the ship began to sink. There was no storm, and there was nothing wrong with the ship, but it sank right then and there. Why did it sink?

Hint: It belongs in the ocean, but you might not call it a ship.

Question 2: Often talked of but never seen. Always coming but never here. It sounds like an idea, but it is just a dream. Still approaching and coming near. You close your eyes, hoping to see me soon. But when you wake up, you realize I'm as far out of your reach as the moon.

Hint: You talk about it today, but it never arrives because it is always today.

Question 3: I weaken everyone for hours each day. I can show you strange and wonderful sights while you're with me. I take you by night and let you go during the day. You don't mind having me, but you will suffer without me.

Hint: Without it, dreaming would be hard.

Question 4: A man was sitting in a car when he saw in front of him a gold door, a silver door, and a bronze door. Which door will he open first?

Question 5: Who has a neck but no head, two arms but no hands, travels from place to place but can't walk or run?

Question 6: You can't see it, and you can't feel it. It can't be heard or smelled. It lies behind the stars, in deep caves under the hills, and empty holes it fills. It's the last thing you see because with it, you can't see at all. What is it?

Question 7: While on my way to St. Ives, I saw a man with his wife. They had seven children and each one had a cat. Each cat had a kitten and each kitten was in a sack. How many people were going to St. Ives?

Question 8: A cloud was my mother, but I didn't stay with her for very long. The wind is my father, but he pushed us away. My son is the cool stream, and he is the reason I exist. I fall once in my life before I sleep in the earth one last time. What am I?

Hint: It's wet and makes you want to stay inside.

Question 9: I will make mountains crumble and temples fall. I've been here since the beginning, and I'll be here long after the end. No one can escape me, and some will say they don't have enough of me. What am I?

Hint: We use a clock to tell it.

Question 10: You can find me in socks, scarves, and mittens, but you can also find me in the paws of a playful kitten. What am I?

Question 11: It is old and has run for a long time. It doesn't move at all. It has a mighty loud roar but no mouth or throat. It is the true beauty and power of nature. What is it?

Hint: You can find it feeding a running river.

Question 12: A ball has fallen into a hole. The hole is a little bigger than the ball, and the hole is deeper than the length of your arm. How will you get the ball out of the hole?

Hint: Balls float!

Question 13: I have four sides and four right angles. I'm part of the quadrilateral family. Do you know what shape I am?

Question 14: I am a body part. In fact, I am two. I share the same name as a type of length, and I fit inside shoes. What am I?

Question 15: I can save a memory forever, but fire can end my life. I've been around for a while, but I probably won't go out of style. What am I?

Hint: Say cheese and snap!

Question 16: What walks on four legs when it's young, two legs when it's older, and three legs when it's near-death?

Hint: The third leg is not attached to them.

Question 17: A farmer hires some help to carry grain to his barn. The farmer carried one sack of grain to the barn while his helper carried only two sacks. Who did the most work?

Read the sentence carefully before you answer. Hint: The helper might not be carrying what you think he's carrying.

Question 18: Two people went for a walk on a cloudy day, but they forgot to bring their umbrellas. Why aren't they getting wet?

Question 19: I'm the start of awesome. You can find me at the end of a comma. I'm also in the middle of a stomach. What am I?

Question 20: What do you call a man that lives in disguise, keeps a lot of secrets, and tells nothing but lies? Will you call him a liar? No, because it's his job. He has no choice if he wants to protect the ones he loves. What would you call him?

Hint: It rhymes with the words lie and fly.

Question 21: You are driving a bus. At the first stop, two women get on. At the second stop, three men get on and one woman gets off. At the third stop, a mom gets on with her three kids. It's raining outside and the bus is bright green. Do you know what color the bus driver's hair is?

Question 22: A boy is walking down the road with a doctor. The boy is the doctor's son, but the doctor is not the boy's father. Who is the doctor?

Question 23: Two fathers and two sons went fishing together. They all caught one fish, but when they came home, there were only three fish. Why is this?

Hint: One of them can be two things. They aren't only a father or a son.

Question 24: There is a man who lives on the top floor of a 24-floor apartment building. Every day he rides the elevator down to the first floor and then he walks to work. When he comes home, he rides the elevator halfway up and uses the stairs to get to the top floor. He does this every day unless there is someone in the elevator with him. Why?

Hint: The elevator button for the top floor must be really high.

Question 25: Mike is a butcher. He is really big. He's 7 feet tall, wears really big boots, and he has a big, bushy beard. What does he weigh?

Question 26: Just before you go to sleep every night, you tell me what to do. Every morning before you wake, I do what I am told, yet I can never escape your scold. What am I?

Hint: It makes a loud noise and is the reason you can get up early in the morning.

Question 27: There is a group of three in everyone's house. One of the groups only sits down and never gets up or moves. The second group eats and breaths and never gets enough of it. The third group goes away and never comes back. What are they?

Hint: You can use one and two to cook food and three appears when food is burnt.

Question 28: I'm the beginning of eternity and at the end of time and space. I am the beginning of every end, and I am the end of every place. What am I?

Hint: Read each word carefully.

Question 29: Mat's mom had a lot of children. She had twelve in total. Their names are January, February, March, April, May, June, July, August, September, and November. What was the last child's name?

Question 30: A man made a promise to his village that one day he would be able to walk on water. Each day he tried, it was warm and sunny, but each day he failed. One day he woke up and it was cold outside. It had been cold all night and he knew that today was his chance. He did it. He walked on water in front of his whole village. How did he do this?

Those riddles were long and challenging, but I knew you could handle them. Let's take a well-deserved break and answer some short and simple questions. Some of these questions may seem a bit strange, but that's where the fun comes from.

Short, Simple, and Strange:

Question 1: Who is that strange thing living in the sea? He has eight arms but no legs, so who is he?

Question 2: The one who has this cannot keep it. It is any shape or size and was bought to be given away. What is it?

Question 3: How do you divide 10 apples between 11 people?

Question 4: What instrument plays from the heart?

Question 5: I'm like a dog with a wagging tail and a furry body, but I am not a dog. What am I?

Question 6: What is Medusa's favorite cheese?

Question 7: What didn't Adam and Eve have that everyone else does?

Question 8: Why does a light shine?

Question 9: What islands should have good singers?

Question 10: Which is the oldest tree?

Question 11: What is a pirate's favorite word?

Question 12: A man has 9 children. Half of his children are boys. How?

Question 13: When is a man like a snake?

Question 14: What kind of money do vampires use?

Question 15: What does a stone become when it's in water?

Question 16: What is always invisible and never out of sight?

Question 17: Where did a rooster crow when all of the world heard him?

Question 18: What type of drum can you not play?

Question 19: When is a ship at sea and not on the water?

Question 20: How can you be sure the engine in a car isn't missing?

Question 21: When are eyes not eyes?

Question 22: What animal likes doors?

Question 23: What country would you send someone to if they had a big appetite?

Question 24: Can you spell enemy with only three letters?

Question 25: What is the largest room in the world?

Question 26: What spends the day at a window, goes to the table for a meal, and then hides away at night?

Question 27: There are thirty white horses on a hill. First they champ, then they stamp, and then they stand still.

Question 28: Can you make six into an odd number?

Question 29: What water can you eat and chew on?

Question 30: What bee can you pass around that doesn't sting?

Question 31: Why don't famous people sweat?

Question 32: What kind of table doesn't have legs?

Question 33: What is red, bloody, and smells like an orange?

Question 34: How can you drop an egg so it never breaks?

Question 35: How many seconds are there in January?

Question 36: What is the smartest letter in the alphabet?

Question 37: What can be green, red, and yellow at the same time?

Question 38: What do you get if you have 2 blackberries and 5 apples?

Question 39: Kids and a monster love me. I'm round and brown. What am I?

Question 40: What can you find here, there, and everywhere?

Question 41: What tastes better than it smells?

Question 42: What cannot talk but will always reply when it is spoken to?

Question 43: What kind of cheese is made backwards?

Question 44: How do you make the number one disappear?

Question 45: What can an elephant have that no one else can?

Question 46: What has one head, one foot, and four legs?

Question 47: Can you name four days of the week that start with the letter T?

Question 48: What nuts can you hang a picture on?

Question 49: What can you hold without touching it?

Question 50: What do you call bears with no ears?

Question 51: Three people said Bill was their brother. Bill said he had no brothers. Who was lying?

Question 52: If you took two apples from three apples, how many apples would you have?

Question 53: Spell me forwards and I am pretty heavy, spell me backwards and I am not. What am I?

Question 54: I saw a boat full of people and yet there wasn't a single person on the boat. How is this possible?

Question 55: What begins with an E, ends with an E, and only carries one letter in it?

Question 56: How many bricks would it take to finish a building made from bricks?

Question 57: There is an electric train going north at 80 mph and the wind is blowing west at 10 mph. Which way will the smoke from the train blow?

Question 58: If it took eight men 10 hours to build a wall, how long will it take four men to build it?

Question 59: Is it illegal for a man to marry his widow's sister?

Question 60: How often can you subtract the number 10 from 100?

Question 61: How many times does the letter A appear between 0 and 100?

Question 62: Where do fish keep their money?

Question 63: Why is it illegal for a man to be buried in California if he is living in New York?

Question 64: Eskimos are good hunters, so why do they not hunt penguins?

Question 65: It goes in dry and comes out wet. The longer it stays in, the stronger it will get. What is it?

Question 66: A peacock can't lay any eggs, so how do they get peacock babies?

Question 67: What is bought by the yard and worn by the foot?

Question 68: What question must always be answered with "Yes"?

Question 69: She is pregnant every time you see her, but she will never give birth. Who is she?

Question 70: What do you call a French person who has golden yellow skin?

Those questions were sticky and tricky indeed, but we got past them with ease. We're learning so much and getting smarter along the way. I hope you're ready for things to get even harder. Those might have been short and strange, but they were also pretty simple. I bet you managed to figure them all out without even scratching your head. You're smarter than riddles like that.

Answers:

Question 1: Stop imagining!

Question 2: The letter M.

Question 3: Wet. If you want it to turn red you can paint it.

Question 4: A milk truck.

Question 5: A palm.

Question 6: A can't opener.

Question 7: A fence.

Question 8: When it's ajar.

Question 9: Bread! If you didn't say toast, well done.

Question 10: On a map.

Take a Hint:

Question 1: Wrong.

Question 2: An elephant's shadow.

Question 3: An anchor.

Question 4: You'd be in 2nd place.

Question 5: A needle.

Question 6: A piano?

Question 7: The match!

Question 8: He has nine left.

Question 9: Mt. Everest. It still existed even though we hadn't discovered it yet.

Question 10: A sponge.

Question 11: An ice cube.

Question 12: A comb.

Question 13: A refrigerator.

Question 14: Your teeth.

Question 15: Hot is faster because you can catch a cold.

Question 16: Short. When you add E and R it becomes shorter.

Question 17: A cloud! It's made of gaseous water.

Question 18: There is no dirt in a hole. It's all been dug out.

Question 19: None. It was Noah's ark.

Question 20: Take away the 's' and seven becomes even.

Question 21: The number zero.

Question 22: Because you stop looking for it when you find it.

Question 23: He slept during the night.

Question 24: A coat of paint.

Question 25: A die.

Question 26: Because you can see right through them.

Question 27: A river.

Question 28: An umbrella!

Question 29: Tuesday paid the bill.

Question 30: Because it was a bright sunny day.

<u>What Is It?</u>

Question 1: The dark.

Question 2: A shadow.

Question 3: A coffin.

Question 4: Racecar.

Question 5: A button.

Question 6: Nobody knows. Do you get it?

Question 7: Water.

Question 8: Shade.

Question 9: A crane.

Question 10: A clock.

Question 11: A cup of tea.

Question 12: The sky.

Question 13: Nightfall.

Question 14: The break of dawn.

Question 15: An alligator.

Question 16: The moon.

Question 17: A lock!

Question 18: A snowflake.

Question 19: A bubble.

Question 20: The wind.

Question 21: A prisoner.

Question 22: An onion!

Question 23: Death.

Question 24: A ruler!

Question 25: Sign language. Do you get it? Because we don't speak sign language, we use our hands.

Question 26: A mirror!

Question 27: A blackboard.

Question 28: It is smoke.

Question 29: A glove!

Question 30: A kitten.

Think Twice Before You Answer:

Question 1: Because he Neverlands!

Question 2: The letter G.

Question 3: Because all of her students were so bright.

Question 4: Because he wanted to go to high school.

Question 5: A mongoose!

Question 6: Are you sleeping?

Question 7: Because he had nobody to go with.

Question 8: Because he wanted to see a butterfly.

Question 9: Through the world wide web of course.

Question 10: Because he was only on the first step.

Question 11: He was feeling a bit crummy.

Question 12: He was a great web designer!

Question 13: An upside-down centipede.

Question 14: The answer to the riddle is gone.

Question 15: Look closely. The word forth is misspelled. It should be fourth. So it doesn't belong.

Question 16: Because it was rated 'Arrrgg.'

Question 17: He wanted to listen to some sole music.

Question 18: A pair of shoes.

Question 19: A platypus!

Question 20: A rainbow!

Question 21: A blade of grass.

Question 22: Beauty, because beauty is in the eye of the bee-holder. Get it?

Question 23: A parrot!

Question 24: A phone.

Question 25: A baby shower.

Question 26: Your height!

Question 27: It can only run halfway because after that, it would be running out of the woods.

Question 28: Corn on a cob!

Question 29: A pair of pants.

Question 30: An embarrassed zebra!

Long Riddles:

Question 1: The submarine captain ordered his crew to dive.

Question 2: The future!

Question 3: Sleep.

Question 4: The car door.

Question 5: A shirt!

Question 6: The dark.

Question 7: Just me. I was the only one going to St. Ives.

Question 8: I am rain.

Question 9: I am time.

Question 10: Yarn!

Question 11: A waterfall.

Question 12: Fill the hole with water and the ball will float to the top. You can also try to find someone with longer arms.

Question 13: I am a square!

Question 14: Feet.

Question 15: A picture.

Question 16: A person. We crawl on all fours when we're babies. We walk on two legs when we're older. When we're really old, we need help walking so we use a cane as a third leg.

Question 17: The farmer did the most work. He carried a sack of grain while the helper just carried two sacks. They were empty.

Question 18: I never said that it was raining.

Question 19: The letter 'A'.

Question 20: He is a spy just like James Bond.

Question 21: You're the bus driver! Remember? What color is your hair?

Question 22: The doctor is the boy's mother.

Question 23: There were only three of them. A man, his son, and his father. He is both a son and a father, which means there are two sons and two fathers.

Question 24: The man was too short to reach the button for the top floor. If someone was with him, then he would ask them to push it. His only other choice was to press the highest button he could reach and use the stairs to get to the top floor.

Question 25: Meat! Mike is a butcher so he weighs meat.

Question 26: An alarm clock.

Question 27: Stove, fire, and smoke.

Question 28: The letter 'E'.

Question 29: The last child was named Mat.

Question 30: It was so cold overnight that the water had frozen over. He was walking on a frozen lake.

Short, Simple, and Strange:

Question 1: An octopus!

Question 2: A gift.

Question 3: You make applesauce!

Question 4: The lungs.

Question 5: A puppy!

Question 6: Gorgonzola.

Question 7: Parents.

Question 8: Because someone turned it on.

Question 9: The Canary Islands.

Question 10: The elder tree.

Question 11: "Arrgg!"

Question 12: All of them are boys. One half are boys and so are the other half.

Question 13: When he is rattled.

Question 14: Blood money!

Question 15: Wet. It becomes wet.

Question 16: The letter 'I' is in both words.

Question 17: On Noah's Ark.

Question 18: A conundrum!

Question 19: When it's on fire.

Question 20: You open the hood and check.

Question 21: When the wind makes them water.

Question 22: A dormouse I would imagine.

Question 23: Hungary!

Question 24: FOE.

Question 25: The room for improvement.

Question 26: A fly!

Question 27: Teeth! The white horses are your teeth and the red hill is your gums.

Question 28: Yes you can. You take away the 's,' then we have IX which are the roman numerals for the number 9.

Question 29: Ice water.

Question 30: A frisbee.

Question 31: Because they have so many fans.

Question 32: A multiplication table.

Question 33: A blood orange.

Question 34: First you have to hard boil it and then drop it on a bed.

Question 35: Only one. The 2nd of January.

Question 36: The letter 'A' because it is the highest grade.

Question 37: A bowl of green, red, and yellow apples.

Question 38: A house of gadgets.

Question 39: A cookie!

Question 40: The word 'here'. It's in all of those words.

Question 41: Your tongue!

Question 42: An echo. It always talks back.

Question 43: Edam is a type of cheese and it is Made spelled backwards.

Question 44: You add a 'G' to it and it's now Gone.

Question 45: A baby elephant!

Question 46: A bed! You can be at the head of the bed or the foot of the bed, and a bed has four legs it stands on.

Question 47: Tuesday, Thursday, Today, and Tomorrow.

Question 48: A walnut of course.

Question 49: You can hold a conversation with someone.

Question 50: B. Get it? Because you took ears away from bears you're left with just 'b'.

Question 51: No one. The three people were Bill's sisters.

Question 52: Two. The two that you took, duh!

Question 53: A ton. A ton is heavy but spelled backwards it becomes not.

Question 54: All the people on the boat were couples. That's so cute!

Question 55: An envelope.

Question 56: Only one. The last brick they have.

Question 57: It's an electric train, there is no smoke.

Question 58: No time at all because the wall is already built.

Question 59: No it's not, but it might be hard to do considering he is dead.

Question 60: Once. After the first time, you'll be subtracting 10 from 90 and so on.

Question 61: Zero times.

Question 62: The Riverbank.

Question 63: Because he's still living. You can't bury someone who's alive.

Question 64: Because Eskimos live in the North Pole and penguins can only be found at the South Pole.

Question 65: A teabag.

Question 66: The peahens lay the eggs.

Question 67: A carpet!

Question 68: What does y-e-s spell?

Question 69: The full moon.

Question 70: A French fry.

Chapter 3

Only for the Brave:

Only for the brave is right. These riddles are difficult and mean, but we aren't scared, are we? We're brave and ready to figure these out. I'll be with you the whole way, ready with hints and clues, not that you need any of those things.

Question 1:

She's the head of a hive, and on a chessboard is where she can be seen;

She's also a card in a deck and that means that she must be...

This riddle is one that rhymes. Find the answer and you'll finish the rhyme. Rhyming riddles are fun and they sound nice. They might be a little hard, but you'll get the hang of them once you give it a try.

Question 2:

I'm found on people's faces as something that they wear;

I help correct bad eyesight, and I always come as a pair.

Question 3:

You often need at least two of these if you want to play a game;

They're covered in spots and are rolled, so can you tell me, what's their name?

Question 4:

If you want to go up to another floor in a building then you may use an escalator;

Another way, of course, is called an…

Question 5:

Oz had good ones from the north and south and wicked ones from the east and west;

But flying around on a broomstick is probably how they are known best.

Question 6:

If you are in a creepy house and hear an unusual sound;

It might be this apparition who can be seen floating around.

Question 7:

This body has no ears or tongue so he's not able to use phones;

Tickling doesn't work on him because he's only made of bones.

Question 8:

I'm something that can be pumped, but I'm not a tire;

I am a body fluid that is drunk by a vampire.

Question 9:

Remove the seeds and carve an orange face;

Your front doorstep is where it's placed.

Question 10:

To make sure you don't have bad luck and that everything will be fine;

Make sure your path is not crossed by this black as night feline.

Riddles are fun, and they're even more fun when they rhyme. I just can't get enough of them.

Question 11:

My wings are used as flippers, so in the water I can flow;

I cannot fly in the air, but I like to slide on snow.

Question 12:

With red and white stripes, it is something that you lick;

Despite the fact that it looks like a hockey stick.

Question 13:

I can come in three forms, but this is my solid state;

And when I'm hard enough, on me you can skate.

Question 14:

Before there were cars and trains, this was how people got around;

They'd get up on a saddle, take the reins, and then the hooves would pound.

Question 15:

If you travel on one of these, an astronaut you must be;

Because it takes you to outer space, where there is zero gravity.

Question 16:

It's dropping from the sky and is more beautiful than rain;

There are no two pieces that will ever look the same.

Question 17:

In a bowl you need to use a spoon, on a cone you can lick;

This frozen dairy dessert has many flavors for you to pick.

Question 18:

It comes in white, milk, dark. This is something you might eat;

As a type of candy, nothing can compete.

Question 19:

Some types slither on the ground while others can live up in the trees;

Adders, vipers, and cobras, what kind of animals are these?

Question 20:

You'll never see one of these if you stay in the daylight;

Beware for when the nighttime comes, your neck might feel a bite.

Question 21:

It's extinct or dormant or active, maybe;

With lava and magma what could this thing be?

Question 22:

It spins at 1,000 miles per hour, but it's not a fairground ride;

At its center, there is a molten core and it's made of crust on the outside.

Question 23:

You can't see me, trust me you can't;

But I can surround everyone, even you and your aunt.

Question 24:

Whether you need to wash some dishes or just your face;

You are going to use this space.

Question 25:

I look like a dog, but dogs don't travel in a pack like me;

I can be vicious so you better watch your back around me.

Question 26:

With me you can draw a pretty picture and that's because of my fine tip. I can break easily and sometimes I'll go dull;

Until there is nothing left of me, null.

Question 27:

I can be all kinds of bright colors, yellow, green, and blue;

If you want, you can mix me together to make a new hue.

Question 28:

You eat me for breakfast. I'm boxed and rather dry;

Grab the bowl, the milk, and a spoon. Unless it's me, that mom forgot to buy.

Question 29:

I happen after a flash, but I'm not a photograph;

You hear me rumbling in a bad storm. I'm lightning's other half.

Question 30:

I'm something that gets stamped, but it's not a foot that steps on me;

In me a letter can be placed for delivery.

It's true that rhymes are fun, but sometimes they can put you off. You can get too caught up in the rhyme and forget what the question was. There's an easy fix for that. What if the answer to the question rhymed with something in the question?

Find the Rhyme:

Question 1: I'm something you use to slide down a snowy hill, and my name rhymes with bed. What am I?

Question 2: I'm a soft and funny tasting fruit. My name rhymes with air.

Question 3: We're small, furry, and a little cute. Our name rhymes with something called dice.

Question 4: I'm tall, brown, and green. I'm covered with leaves and my name rhymes with bee.

Question 5: You keep me on your wrist so you can tell the time. I rhyme with a soldiers march.

Question 6: I have two wheels, pedals, and a chain. I can take you anywhere you want to go, and I rhyme with Mike.

Question 7: I'm small and black, and I sleep upside down in caves. I'm nothing like them, but my name rhymes with cat.

Question 8: I can be any number from 1 to 10. I have a funny shape and I rhyme with late.

Question 9: You wear me on your body but only when it's cold outside. I rhyme with packet.

Question 10: You like to play me when you're bored. I rhyme with lame, but I am anything but.

Question 11: I'm still unless you disturb me. I'm made of water and I'm home to many things. I'm beautiful indeed, but my name rhymes with snake.

Question 12: You may have seen your mom and dad do this once or twice. It's lovely and nice. When you're young, it looks gross. It rhymes with bliss.

Question 13: I can be bright and dark if you want me to. You use me to paint and draw. I'm a color if you haven't guessed yet, and I rhyme with new.

Question 14: I'm a bird that floats on the water. When I have babies, they trail behind me and we stick our heads underwater for food. I rhyme with luck.

Question 15: I'm what you see in the bathroom. You see me every morning and every night. I look like you, but I'm not, and I rhyme with protection.

Question 16: People drink me in the morning before they go to work. I'm a bitter, powerful drink that gives them energy. My name rhymes with toffee.

Question 17: He wears a pointy hat and carries a staff. He does magic and his name rhymes with his pet lizard.

Question 18: We go to it every day except two, and it's important if we want to learn. It's not as fun, but its name rhymes with pool.

Question 19: It takes you to many places while staying in one spot. There are many adventures to be had in its pages. You can touch and you can look because that's what it rhymes with.

Question 20: I'm small and fragile with wings of red and white. I'm pretty and my name rhymes with shady slug.

I didn't give you a clue or hint for those because I knew you wouldn't need them. Remember to read the question carefully and think outside of the box. The answer can be found in the question if you look hard enough.

Think Hard:

Question 1: What always ends everything?

Question 2: What age is someone in their fifth prime?

Hint: Do you remember what a prime is?

Question 3: Where can your best friend sit, but you can't?

Hint: It's not on your lap, but very close.

Question 4: What letter in the alphabet can make an old coin more valuable?

 Hint: It's not the coin you're making more valuable.

Question 5: OOTTFFSS…What are the next 3 letters?

Hint: The letters are the first letters for certain words.

Question 6: Re-arrange the letters, OOUSWTDNEJR, to spell just one word.

Hint: Read carefully.

Question 7: You carry it everywhere you go, but it never gets heavy.

Hint: It's not your shadow. In fact, it's nothing you can see, touch, or hold, but you can hear it.

Question 8: If a chicken says, 'All chickens are liars,' is the chicken telling the truth?

Question 9: What bird can be heard during mealtimes?

Question 10: Do you know what word contains three consecutive double letters?

Hint: You can find them at a library.

Question 11: I went into the woods and got it. I wasn't looking for it, I just sat down and it was there. I brought it home with me because I couldn't find it. What is it?

Hint: It starts with an 'S' and is made of tiny wood.

Question 12: Glittering points that thrust directly downward. They are sparkling spears that can never rust. What is it?

Hint: Sharp, solid water.

Question 13: What is it that is deaf, dumb, and blind but always tells the truth?

Hint: It copies you.

Question 14: Crimson I am born, yellow I dance, ebony I die.

Hint: If you touch it, you burn.

Question 15: How many birthdays does the average man have?

Hint: Look carefully. The hint is in the space between words.

Question 16: I can have all the colors of the rainbow or have no color at all. I can be empty, and I can be full. What am I?

 Hint: You drink from me.

Question 17: Inside a dark tunnel lies an iron beast. It can only attack when pulled back. What is it?

Hint: The iron beast makes a noise, like a loud bang, when it is released.

Question 18: More of me is hidden and less of me is seen. I can take down ships if they cross my path, but I'm peaceful as I float through my endless blue world.

Hint: This is not the Titanic's friend.

Question 19: Take one and scratch its head. It once was red, but now it is black instead. What is it?

Hint: You can't light a candle without it.

Question 20: My voice can be heard from far or near. I can be smaller than your hand and bigger than your house. The noise I make all depends on how hard you ring me. What am I?

Hint: One of my names is Big Ben.

Question 21: What is as deep as a cup but even a river can't fill it up?

Hint: It has holes in it.

Question 22: Why is the best baker most in want of bread?

Question 23: Can you spell water with only three letters?

Question 24: How many black beans will make five white ones?

Hint: What does a black bean look like on the inside?

Question 25: What letters of the alphabet are the busiest?

Question 26: Black within, red without, with four corners, roundabout. What is it?

Hint: Start a fire in me and Santa won't come visit.

Question 27: Why are your nose and chin always at variance?

Hint: It's because of your mouth.

Question 28: What can you divide but cannot see where it is divided?

Hint: It sounds like a math question, but it's not.

Question 29: When is a boat like a knife?

Question 30: Why is a conundrum like a monkey?

Question 31: I have four legs and I have no tail. Usually, you can hear me at night, and I like to hop. What am I?

Hint: I'm also green and I eat flies.

Question 32: What did the turkey say to the rooster when he challenged him to a fight?

Question 33: What kind of music do rabbits like?

Question 34: I travel very slowly when gliding along the ground. Your garden is where my shell and I are found. What am I?

Hint: I hate salt.

Question 35: I'm known as the king of the jungle and this is where I reign with my large teeth and mane. What am I?

Question 36: A dog is on a 10-foot chain but wants something 12 feet away from him. How does he get it?

Think outside the box before you answer.

Question 37: What two keys can't open any doors?

Hint: They're both animals with key in their name.

Question 38: Why do birds fly south for the winter?

Hint: It's the fastest option.

Question 39: How many letters are there in the alphabet?

Read that carefully.

Question 40: I RIGHT I; What does this mean?

Hint: What is the right in between?

Question 41: What words look the same backwards and upside down?

Hint: You do it in a pool.

Question 42: A man was taking a walk in the rain with no umbrella and no hat. His clothes were soaked, but none of the hair on his head got wet. How?

Question 43: If you multiply me by any other number, I will always remain the same. What number am I?

Question 44: Why did the pony cough?

Question 45: What creature has two heads, sees with four eyes, walks on six legs, and has a tail?

Hint: It's one thing on top of another.

Question 46: How did the chimp fix the leaky faucet?

Question 47: What did the traffic light say to the car?

Question 48: What did the snowman say to the other snowman?

Question 49: Why can't you give Elsa a balloon?

Question 50: I am something when I am not known, but I am nothing when I am known. What am I?

Hint: It's right in front of you.

You went through those with ease. My hints were probably very helpful, so you're welcome. The ones that rhymed were my favorite. Which ones did you like the most? We can think about that later because there's still more to solve.

Answers:

Question 1: She's a queen.

Question 2: Glasses.

Question 3: Dice.

Question 4: Elevator.

Question 5: A witch!

Question 6: It's a spooky ghost.

Question 7: A skeleton.

Question 8: Blood.

Question 9: It's a pumpkin!

Question 10: A black cat.

Question 11: A penguin.

Question 12: Candy cane!

Question 13: Ice.

Question 14: Horses.

Question 15: It's a spaceship!

Question 16: Snowflake

Question 17: Ice-cream.

Question 18: Chocolate!

Question 19: They're snakes.

Question 20: A vampire.

Question 21: Volcano.

Question 22: The Earth!

Question 23: Gas!

Question 24: A sink.

Question 25: It's a wolf.

Question 26: A pencil.

Question 27: Paint.

Question 28: I am cereal!

Question 29: Thunder.

Question 30: An envelope.

Find the Rhyme:

Question 1: A sled.

Question 2: A pear.

Question 3: Mice.

Question 4: A tree.

Question 5: A watch.

Question 6: A bike.

Question 7: A bat.

Question 8: The number 8.

Question 9: A jacket.

Question 10: A game.

Question 11: A lake.

Question 12: A kiss.

Question 13: The color blue.

Question 14: A duck.

Question 15: Your reflection.

Question 16: Coffee.

Question 17: A wizard.

Question 18: School.

Question 19: A book.

Question 20: Ladybug.

Think Hard:

Question 1: The letter 'G'!

Question 2: They are only seven, because seven is the fifth prime number.

Question 3: Next to you!

Question 4: The letter 'G'. Add it to old, and you'll get a gold coin.

Question 5: ENT. The sequence contains the first letters of all the numbers from one to ten.

Question 6: 'Just one word'. That's what you can spell when you rearrange the letters.

Question 7: Your name.

Question 8: Chickens can't talk, silly!

Question 9: A Swallow.

Question 10: Bookkeeper.

Question 11: A splinter!

Question 12: Icicles.

Question 13: A mirror, because your reflection never lies.

Question 14: Fire.

Question 15: One. You're only born once.

Question 16: A glass.

Question 17: The dark cave is the chamber of a gun and the iron beast is a bullet.

Question 18: An iceberg.

Question 19: A match.

Question 20: A bell.

Question 21: A kitchen strainer because it has holes in it you can't fill it up.

Question 22: Because he kneads (needs) it the most.

Question 23: Yes you can. Ice - it's a form of water.

Question 24: Five ones when they are peeled.

Question 25: B and C. Get it?

Question 26: It is a chimney.

Question 27: Because there are always words passing between them.

Question 28: Water. You can divide it, but you'll never be able to see where you divided it.

Question 29: When it is a cutter. Some boats are called cutters and they're used on icy oceans to cut through the ice.

Question 30: Because it is full of nonsense.

Question 31: A frog.

Question 32: "Are you chicken?"

Question 33: They like to listen to Hip Hop.

Question 34: I am a snail.

Question 35: I am a lion.

Question 36: The chain isn't attached to anything.

Question 37: A monkey and a donkey.

Question 38: Because it would take too long to walk.

Question 39: Eleven. There are eleven letters in 'the alphabet'.

Question 40: It means right between the eyes.

Question 41: 'Swims' looks the same both backwards and upside down.

Question 42: Because he didn't have any hair.

Question 43: Zero.

Question 44: Because he was a little hoarse. Get it?

Question 45: It's a cowboy riding his horse, of course!

Question 46: With a monkey wrench.

Question 47: "Don't look! I'm changing."

Question 48: "Do you smell carrots?"

Question 49: Because she'll 'let it go' and she'll probably sing while she's doing it.

Question 50: The answer is a riddle.

Chapter 4

Extreme Brainteasers:

These riddles are as the name suggests, extremely brain teasing. They're hard, yes, but you don't have to worry. You've got me, and you've got the hints to help you. We'll make it through these with maybe a few problems. With this chapter you should take your time and think as hard as you can. The best place to think is out of the box. Let's get at them!

Question 1: It's round like an apple and deep like a cup, but not even the king's horses can lift it up or move it. What is it?

Hint: It has a bucket that fetches water from the bottom.

Question 2: If you are in a house that is burning, this thing is best to make before the fire's too big for you to take on. What is it?

Hint: The answer is another word for quickly or fast.

Question 3: At the sound of me, men may dream or stomp their feet. At the sound of me, they may even laugh or weep. What am I?

Hint: It plays on the radio or TV for you to sing or dance along to.

Question 4: Long and silky like a trout, it never sings till its guts come out. What is it?

Hint: When it sings, it's quite loud. Its favorite song is a big BANG!

Question 5: How did the court know the judge was ready for bed?

Hint: He was wearing something you wear in court and to bed.

Question 6: What animal has no wings yet will fly?

Hint: It's small and ugly at first, but after it takes a long nap it will be beautiful.

Question 7: Did you hear about the soldier who bought a camouflage sleeping bag?

Question 8: How do you communicate with a monster that lives on the seabed?

Hint: You need a line.

Question 9: I can build small castles. I can tear down a mountain. I have the ability to make some men blind, and in one of my forms, I can help others see. What am I?

Hint: You can find a lot of it by the beach.

Question 10: What did the paper say to the pen?

Question 11: There is a forest somewhere on Earth. The only life in this forest consists of the trees growing there. A storm came and made one of the trees fall. What sound did it make?

Hint: Remember, no one was there to hear it...

Question 12: He's about the size of a squash, and he robs the whole village. What is he?

Hint: He is round and furry with a long pink tail.

Question 13: When is the best time to have lunch?

Question 14: Who are the two brothers that live on opposite sides of the street but never see each other?

Hint: The street is your face.

Question 15: What word can you take away the whole and still have some leftover?

Hint: It is a word. Read carefully.

Question 16: You search for me when you get sick, and when you need the toilet, I'm the first room you pick. What room am I?

This one sounds really easy right? Probably because it is.

Question 17: What do zebras have in common?

Question 18: A leaf that bears a fruit that bears a leaf. What is it?

Hint: The first part of the word is a tree and the second part is a small, sweet fruit.

Question 19: Why is a cook bad?

Hint: He often beats something.

Question 20: God's arrows cannot be counted.

Hint: It's wet and it falls from the heavens.

Those were really difficult, it's a good thing we had those hints. Let's take a break from the riddles and questions and try something else. Let's try out a few things that will twist and tie your tongue up in knots.

Tongue Twisters:

Try saying these as fast as you can and see who can say it the fastest.

1: A big bug bit the little beetle, but the little beetle bit the big bug back.

2: How much wood could a woodchuck chuck if a woodchuck could chuck wood.

3: Toy boat. Toy boat. Toy boat.

4: If two witches were watching two watches: Which witch would watch which watch?

5: No need to light a night-light on a light night like tonight.

6: If a dog chews shoes, whose shoes does he choose?

7: Double bubble gum bubbles double.

8: Fresh French fried fly fritters.

9: Which wrist watches and Swiss wristwatches?

10: The cat catchers can't catch caught cats.

11: Fred fed Ted bread and Ted fed Fred bread.

12: Daddy draws doors. Daddy draws doors.

13: Green glass globes glow greenly.

14: She sees cheese.

15: Can you can a can as a canner can can a can?

16: Twelve twins twirled twelve twigs.

17: How many yaks could a yak pack pack if a yak pack could pack yaks?

18: Fuzzy Wuzzy was a bear. Fuzzy Wuzzy had no hair. Fuzzy Wuzzy wasn't very fuzzy was he?

19: Clean clams crammed in clean cans.

20: Six sticky skeletons.

That was tongue twisting fun for everybody. Try challenging each other to see who can say a tongue twister the fastest. How many times can you say one until you mess up?

Did you like the rhyming riddles as much as I did? Here's a few more.

Rhyme that Riddle:

Question 1:

After a fall, I take over. Then life does stall or at least grows slower.

Question 2:

I touch the earth, and I touch the sky. If I touch you, once you'll surely die.

Question 3:

I dance in the wind, and I bow to the storm. I grow best in temperatures that are warm. By the riverbeds, I like to grow where the people in boats like to row.

Question 4:

What has roots that no one sees and can climb higher than the tallest trees? Up, up, up it goes, but it never grows.

Question 5:

What word ruins the rhyme and doesn't belong:

That, hat, mat, cat, what, sat, pat, or chat.

Question 6:

I'm very good at concealing from you what is real, and I'm excellent at hiding what is true. Sometimes I can bring out the confidence in you.

Question 7:

Strip off my skin, and my flesh is what you'll reveal. It tastes sweet and tart once you throw away the peel.

Question 8:

Try to beat me and try in vain. When I win, I will end the pain.

Question 9:

They made me a mouth and long orange nose but didn't give me breath. Frozen water gives me life, but fire brings me a wet death.

Question 10:

You might find me in a tree. I'm the one moving really slowly. I share a name with one of the sins, but from them I am free.

A Hint or Two for You:

Question 1: I am a big threat to humanity, but you wouldn't get rid of me even if you could. What am I?

Hint: The answer is in the question, and it's you and me.

Question 2: Smell me, buy me, and deliver me. I won't change.

Hint: These three words sound the same but are spelled differently and mean different things.

Question 3: Who builds his things stronger than a carpenter's wood, a blacksmith's metals, and a baker's bread?

Hint: The things he builds are built to last forever in the ground.

Question 4: A town only has one barber. The barber only shaves people who do not shave themselves. So who shaves the barber?

Hint: The barber cannot shave themselves because the barber only shaves people who don't shave themselves.

Question 5: Why are manholes round instead of square?

Question 6: I'm not a pool, but I have a cover. I'm not a tree, but I have leaves. I'm not a slave, but I am bound. I'm not a website, but I have pages. I'm not a shirt, but I have sleeves. What am I?

Hint: I have stories, as well.

Question 7: Under pressure is the only way I work, and by myself is the only way I'm hurt. What am I?

Hint: It's a girl's best friend.

Question 8: There are ten soldiers in white dead on a wooden floor. They were struck down by a black monster with three eyes. What happened?

Hint: This is a game.

Question 9: It is always right in front of you, but you cannot see it no matter how hard you look. What is it?

Hint: It's not tomorrow, but it's similar.

Question 10: It is weightless, but it can be seen. If it is put in a barrel of water, it will make it lighter. What is it?

Hint: You can have it in the ground and in your pocket, too.

Question 11: It can go up and down the stairs, and it does this without moving. What is it?

Hint: You put it on the floor and walk all over it.

Question 12: I know a word with three letters that if you add two more letters, then less there will be.

Hint: This word is another for little.

Question 13: Someone will write me, someone will speak about me, someone will expose me, and I can be broken.

Hint: Your parents watch it on TV and read it in the newspaper.

Question 14: Do you know what is black, white, and read all over?

Hint: See the above hint for the answer.

Question 15: There's a word I know that has six letters, but if you remove one letter, then only twelve remain.

Hint: This word is usually used for ordering more than a few eggs.

Question 16: When things go wrong, what can you always count on?

Question 17: If you have four cups of sugar in front of you and you take two away, how many will you have?

Question 18: If I am broken, I do not stop working. If I am touched, I may be snared. If I am lost, then nothing else will matter. What am I?

Hint: It lives in your chest.

Question 19: What did the fish say when he ran into a concrete wall?

Question 20: How do you double something that's in your hand the easiest and fastest way?

Hint: It has to fit in your hand because you have to hold it up to something.

Question 21: What has four eyes but can never see?

Hint: It's not a person, but a place, and its eyes are not like yours or mine.

Question 22: What would a tall chimney say to a short chimney?

Question 23: What do you need to spot a building 20 miles away?

Question 24: Which animal sleeps with its shoes on?

Question 25: What clothes do a house wear?

Question 26: Sometimes I shine and sometimes I'm dull. I can be big, and I can be small. I can be pointed or curved, and although I'm very sharp, don't ask me any questions for I won't answer them. What am I?

Hint: It lives in the kitchen and is used to cut or carve.

Question 27: A limo driver was going down a one-way street the wrong way. He passed several police officers who didn't stop or arrest him. Why not?

Question 28: I have wings, and I am able to fly. I am not a bird, but I soar high in the sky. What am I?

Hint: People can ride inside it.

Question 29: Let's say that four people would be able to repair four bicycles in only four hours. If that is true, then how many bicycles will eight people repair in only eight hours.

Hint: Do the math!

Question 30: I can be a person, I can be a fruit, and I can also be a bird. What am I?

Question 31: Which of the superheroes is terrible at their job? They are always running late and getting lost?

Hint: What sounds like wonder but isn't?

Question 32: What is blue during the day, black at night, but doesn't actually have any color?

Question 33: What is always late and never present now?

Hint: What is late with an extra letter?

Question 34: What can be big, white, dirty, and wicked?

Question 35: If a car key opens a car, and a house key opens a house, then what key opens a banana?

Question 36: What did A say to D when it was looking for E?

Question 37: What has feet inside but no feet outside?

Question 38: Do other countries beside America have the 4th of July?

Question 39: Which part of the day is the easiest to break?

Question 40: Which one doesn't quite belong: vultures, eagles, hawks, pelicans, or ostrich?

Hint: One of them cannot do something the others can.

Question 41: What do Halloween, autumn, Dracula, and August have in common? Pumpkin does not have the same thing in common.

Question 42: What is only five letters long but contains thousands of letters?

Hint: It's a famous book that everyone owns or has read.

Question 43: Which one is not white: The White House, sugar, polar bears, and snow?

Question 44: The rabbit went outside and ran around in the rain, but none of its hair got wet. How is this possible?

Question 45: What do ladybugs and Dalmatians have in common?

Question 46: What is the shortest number: six, three, five, or four?

Question 47: What word in the dictionary is hilarious to say?

Question 48: What did addition say to subtraction when they discovered each other on Facebook?

Question 49: What did the right eyebrow say to the left eyebrow?

Question 5o: You can collect me, flip me, spin me, spend me, and toss me. Everyone around the world has a different version of me. What am I?

Answers:

Question 1: It's a well.

Question 2: Haste!

Question 3: I am music.

Question 4: It's a gun.

Question 5: He's wearing a robe.

Question 6: A caterpillar. It doesn't have wings at first, but soon it will become a butterfly and fly away.

Question 7: He fell asleep in it, and now we can't find him.

Question 8: You drop him a line. That's what old people used to say when they wanted to call someone.

Question 9: Sand.

Question 10: You're always 'Write'.

Question 11: It made no sound. Sound does not exist if no one is there to hear it.

Question 12: He is a rat.

Question 13: After breakfast.

Question 14: Your eyes!

Question 15: The word 'wholesome'. If you take away 'whole', you will still have 'some'.

Question 16: The bathroom.

Question 17: They're stripes!

Question 18: It's a pineapple.

Question 19: Because he beats the eggs.

Question 20: The answer is rain.

<u>Rhyme that Riddle:</u>

Question 1: Death.

Question 2: Lightning.

Question 3: Seaweed.

Question 4: A mountain.

Question 5: The word is 'what' because it isn't pronounced like the others.

Question 6: Makeup.

Question 7: An orange.

Question 8: Death.

Question 9: A snowman.

Question 10: A sloth.

A Hint or Two for You:

Question 1: The answer is humanity itself.

Question 2: Scent, cent, and sent.

Question 3: A coffin maker.

Question 4: The barber is a woman, she doesn't need to shave.

Question 5: Because then the round lids won't fit them anymore.

Question 6: I am a book.

Question 7: A diamond.

Question 8: They are bowling pins, and they were struck down by a bowling ball.

Question 9: The future.

Question 10: A hole.

Question 11: A carpet.

Question 12: The word is 'few'. If you add two letters to it, then it will become fewer, which is less than a few.

Question 13: The News.

Question 14: A Newspaper; it's black, white, and people read it all over.

Question 15: Dozens, which is more than 12, but if you take away the 'S', it is just 12.

Question 16: Your fingers. No matter what, you can count on your fingers.

Question 17: You'll have the one that you took.

Question 18: Your heart.

Question 19: Fish can't talk or run.

Question 20: You hold it up to the mirror, and it is doubled by its reflection.

Question 21: Mississippi. It has four 'I's, but it's the name of a place so it can't see.

Question 22: "Are you old enough to smoke?"

Question 23: You need good eyesight.

Question 24: A horse. It's hooves are its shoes, and they can't take them off.

Question 25: Address. Get it? A dress.

Question 26: A knife.

Question 27: He was walking on the sidewalk, not driving.

Question 28: An airplane.

Question 29: They can repair 16 bicycles.

Question 30: I am Kiwi.

Question 31: Wander Women because she is always wandering around.

Question 32: The Ocean! Water doesn't actually have a color. It's transparent.

Question 33: Later.

Question 34: A lie.

Question 35: A monkey.

Question 36: "Go away, he is BC."

Question 37: Shoes!

Question 38: Yes, they do. They also have the 5th and 6th of July.

Question 39: Breakfast, of course.

Question 40: Ostrich! Because they can't fly and the other birds can.

Question 41: They have the letter 'A' in common.

Question 42: The Bible.

Question 43: Polar bears, because their fur actually has no color.

Question 44: Because rabbits don't have hair, they have fur. His fur got wet.

Question 45: They both have spots!

Question 46: Six, because it has only three letters and the others have more.

Question 47: Hilarious, of course.

Question 48: "Add me."

Question 49: "You look surprised to see me."

Question 50: It's a coin!

Chapter 5

Some Extra Fun:

The tongue twister to twist everyone's tongue:

1: I wish to wish the wish you wish to wish, but if you wish the wish the witch wishes, I won't wish the wish you wish to wish.

The riddle that makes no sense:

Question 2: If I say I am lying, am I telling the truth?

A mystery indeed:

Question 3: A lady is unlocking the door to her round house when she hears someone scream. She goes inside to find her husband dead. The butcher says, "I was chopping meat." The cook says, "I was cooking fish."

The maid says, "I was sweeping the corners." Who killed the husband?

A confusing rhyme:

Question 4: *It can form to make rain, but if you take away one of its legs, then it'll give you only pain.*

This one will make you laugh:

Question 5: What time did the tooth fairy arrive so she could collect the kid's tooth and leave a dollar behind?

Short but not simple:

Question 6: During which month do people end up sleeping less?

Tricky and sticky, indeed:

Question 7: You can drop me from the tallest building and I'll be fine, but if you drop me into water, I will die.

A long and hard one for the road:

Question 8: Imagine you had a green house and inside your green house, you had a white house, and inside that white house, you had a red house, and finally inside that, there were a lot of tiny black babies. What is it?

You won't guess this one:

Question 9: A man is pushing his car down the road when he stops in front of a hotel. He shouts out, "I'm bankrupt!" Why did he do this?

This is not a game to take lightly:

Question 10: There are eight of us on the front line. We always go forth and never go back so we can protect our king from a foe's attack.

Answers:

Question 2: It is a paradox. If someone says they are lying, then they can't be telling the truth because then they won't be lying anymore.

Question 3: The maid killed the husband because her excuse doesn't make sense. She says she was "sweeping the corners," but there are no corners in a round house.

Question 4: The answer is the letter 'R'. 'R' is used to spell Rain, but if you take away one of its legs, it becomes 'P' which is used to spell Pain.

Question 5: She arrived at exactly Tw-ooth 0' clock.

Question 6: February, because there are fewer nights in it.

Question 7: A piece of paper.

Question 8: A watermelon. The outside is green, then there is a white layer, then the red inside, and finally the black small seeds are the babies.

Question 9: Because he was playing Monopoly.

Question 10: Pawns in a game of chess.

Conclusion:

It may be sad, but I'm afraid those are all the riddles I have for now. You were a big help in figuring them out. I told you the answers would be silly and the questions would be ridiculous. Riddles are very sneaky, and tricky, and sticky. The tongue twisters were a treat and the rhymes were great fun, indeed. All journeys must come to an end as must this one. You can always go back to the start and try again. Ignore the hints this time and try on your own.

Show this book to your friends. Ask them the questions and see if they can find the answers. It's always fun to challenge others and see if they're as smart as you. Give them hints if they need them because I'm sure you needed the hints, too.

Remember, if you didn't understand all the questions or you couldn't find all of the answers, that's fine. There's always room for a second chance. It doesn't matter how fast you solve the riddles, it only matters that you solve them eventually. Take your time and read the question as many times as you want before you guess the answer. Keep in mind that most of the time, the answer is in the question itself. You'll get it right. I know you will. You're a smart kid, and no riddle is ever too hard, sticky, or tricky for a smart kid.

Thank you for helping me with the riddles! I hope you had as much fun as me. Don't stop here. Look for more riddles to solve and more fun to be had. Spread the fun with everyone around you, as well. The world of riddles is a big one, and it's ready to be explored. There are lots of caves to poke your head into and rocks to look under. In every corner or shadow, there is a riddle hiding, waiting to be solved. Put on your shoes and get going. Don't forget to look out for those sticky tongue twisters.

References:

203 Fun Riddles for Kids with Answers - Icebreaker Ideas. (2019). Icebreaker Ideas. Retrieved 20 October 2019, from https://icebreakerideas.com/riddles-for-kids/

McKay, B. (2019). 29 Best Riddles for Kids of All Ages | The Art of Manliness. The Art of Manliness. Retrieved 20 October 2019, from https://www.artofmanliness.com/articles/riddles-for-kids/

100 Brain Teasers With Answers for Kids and Adults - Icebreaker Ideas. (2019). Icebreaker Ideas. Retrieved 20 October 2019, from https://icebreakerideas.com/brain-teasers/

Easy Riddles For Kids: 23 Brain Teasers for Fun. (2016). Flintobox. Retrieved 20 October 2019, from https://flintobox.com/blog/child-development/easy-riddles-kids-23-brain-teasers

Page, R., Riddles, N., Riddles, B., Teasers, B., Riddles, C., & Riddles, D. et al. (2019). What is it Riddles Page 22 of 22 Riddles.com. Riddles.com. Retrieved 20 October 2019, from https://www.riddles.com/what-is-it-riddles?page=22

Riddles, D. (2018). 35 Short Riddles - Funny, Tricky & Hard Short Riddles With Answers | Get Riddles. Riddles With Answers for Kids & Adults. Retrieved 21 October 2019, from https://www.getriddles.com/short-riddles/

120 Riddles and Brain Teasers for Kids. (2019). EverythingMom. Retrieved 22 October 2019, from https://www.everythingmom.com/parenting/45-riddles-and-brain-teasers-for-kids

Page, R., Riddles, N., Riddles, B., Teasers, B., Riddles, C., & Riddles, D. et al. (2019). DOES - Riddles.com. Riddles.com. Retrieved 22 October 2019, from https://www.riddles.com/archives/7723

Page, R., Riddles, N., Riddles, B., Teasers, B., Riddles, C., & Riddles, D. et al. (2019). Short Riddles Page 1 of 13 Riddles.com. Riddles.com. Retrieved 22 October 2019, from https://www.riddles.com/short-riddles?page=1

Fun Trick Questions and Brain Teasers That'll Boggle Your Mind. (2019). Plentifun. Retrieved 22 October 2019, from https://plentifun.com/fun-trick-questions-brain-teasers

Pepper, S., Pepper, S., Pepper, S., Pepper, S., & Pepper, S. (2017). Rhyming Riddles | Riddles For Kids. Riddles-for-kids.org. Retrieved 22 October 2019, from http://riddles-for-kids.org/rhyming-riddles/

(2019). Kids.lovetoknow.com. Retrieved 22 October 2019, from https://kids.lovetoknow.com/kids-activities/scavenger-hunt-riddles-kids

100+ Tongue Twisters for Family Fun. (2019). EverythingMom. Retrieved 22 October 2019, from https://www.everythingmom.com/activities/50-tongue-twisters-for-family-fun

5 Rhyming Riddles (With Answers) - ESL Friendly for Online and Classroom - DigiNo. (2019). DigiNo. Retrieved 22 October 2019, from https://digino.org/rhyming-riddles/

Riddles, D. (2018). 43 Funny Riddles - With Answers for Kids & Adults | Get Riddles. Riddles With Answers for Kids & Adults. Retrieved 22 October 2019, from https://www.getriddles.com/funny-riddles/

Riddles, D. (2018). 31 Hard Riddles - With Answers for Adults & Kids | Get Riddles. Riddles With Answers for Kids & Adults. Retrieved 22 October 2019, from https://www.getriddles.com/hard-riddles/

Funny Riddles – Page 12 – Riddles & Answers. (2016). Riddles & Answers. Retrieved 22 October 2019, from https://riddles.fyi/funny-riddles/page/12/

Easy Riddles For Kids With Answers | LaffGaff, Home Of Fun And Laughter. (2019). Laffgaff.com. Retrieved 22 October 2019, from http://laffgaff.com/easy-riddles-for-kids-with-answers/

Made in the USA
Coppell, TX
08 June 2020